Worship Is All of Life

Worship Is All of Life

Robert A. Morey

CHRISTIAN PUBLICATIONS
Camp Hill, Pennsylvania

Christian Publications

Publishing House of
The Christian and Missionary Alliance
3825 Hartzdale Drive
Camp Hill, PA 17011

The mark of ✝ *vibrant faith*

Robert A. Morey is deeply involved
in the evangelical Christian
community. A noted author, he is
also pastor, teacher and scholar.
Among Dr. Morey's published books
are the following:
Death and the Afterlife
The Saving Work of Christ
Is Sunday the Christian Sabbath?
The Bible and Drug Abuse
How to Answer a Mormon
How to Answer a Jehovah's Witness
Horoscopes and the Christian
Reincarnation and Christianity

Contents

Introduction

We are living in a very confusing church age. Because there are so many church denominations and theological traditions, a person can become hopelessly lost in endless debates. Yet, the child of God who sits in the pew has a very simple and practical question: "How does God want me to worship Him?"

A true believer is not interested in speculative theological answers spun out of someone's fantasies. Neither will a dedicated Christian settle for dusty old traditions simply for tradition's sake. The sincere child of God wants to know what the Bible teaches. He or she wants the Scriptures explained and interpreted in a sane and practical way. The Spirit-filled Christian wants the truth, the whole truth and nothing but the truth of Scripture. He really does not care what traditions or previous ideas have to be discarded in order to worship God as He commands in His Word.

I firmly believe that the time has come for the people of God to examine the subject of worship. Why? The people of God are becoming dissatisfied with what is passed off as worship in their churches. They are tired of dull services or services that remind them of the circus.

In one worship service we find total freedom; in another, total form. In one there is confusion;

in the other, absolute order. One kind of worship service is marked by emotionalism and carnal exhibitionism; another is marked by intellectualism and passivity. One is long on experience and short on teaching; another is long on teaching and short on experience.

No wonder Christians are so often confused on how to worship God! Let us determine to study the issue and then to involve ourselves in the holy business of worshiping the one and only Triune God—Father, Son and Holy Spirit.

At this point we encounter a perplexing problem. Everyone professes that he or she wants to go "back to the Bible." But what does it mean to go "back to the Bible"?

I could quickly reply that this means to be "apostolic." But what does "apostolic" mean? The following diagram defines "apostolic":

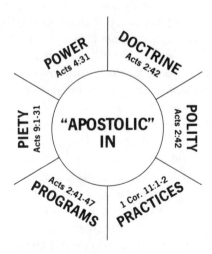

You cannot be apostolic unless you accept the *doctrines* which the apostles set forth in Scripture. In Acts 2:42, we are told that the early Christians were continually "devoting themselves to the apostles' teaching."

Christian doctrine was "once for all delivered to the saints" in the New Testament (Jude 3). Thus it is safe to follow the general rule: If a doctrine is new, it is not true; if it is true, it is not new. This assumption is based on Jude 3 and should deliver us from many of the present-day novel and strange doctrines which do not have any historic or apostolic pedigree.

In order for a church to function in an apostolic way, its *polity* or government must follow the plan set forth by the apostles in Scripture. Many churches have been awakened to the apostolic polity of the plurality of elders and the ministry of true deacons. The distinction between clergy and laity is now being rejected as unbiblical.

The church needs to reestablish relevant apostolic *practices*. For example, the reappearance of the "agape feast" with its warm and dynamic observance of the Lord's Supper is exciting. Concerned Christians are also taking a second look at the social action carried on by the apostolic church because the traditional evangelical church has failed to follow the apostolic practice of ministering to the poor and needy.

To retain the apostolic church order, some of the *programs* which the apostles instituted need to be reestablished. One particular program which is receiving fresh attention is the role of godly women in the discipleship program of the local church. That evangelical women have been ignored and left to shift for themselves except for an occasional sermon on submission is an undeniable reality. If we return to the apostolic discipleship program, Christian women will be given their rightful place once again.

A return to the solid *piety* of the apostles is a must. They were men who believed in holiness. All the modern forms of superficial instant superspirituality would be repugnant to the apostles. They lived a rugged and God-fearing Christian life. If we are going to endure possible future persecutions, we must develop the solid piety of the apostles.

Finally, we need to experience and to demonstrate the *power* that marked the lives of the early Christians. With the forces of darkness rallying for their last great assault on humanity, we had better develop the power of the apostolic Christians. It is dangerous to pretend that we cannot experience or demonstrate the apostolic power of the Holy Spirit in this age. When we are faced with demonic forces, we must have the power of the Holy Spirit.

In light of the above points, we must with shame admit that some evangelical churches and movements have magnified one of the above to the exclusion of the others. Too many Christian groups are running to extremes. They fail to remember that "a half-truth presented as a whole-truth becomes a non-truth."

In opposition to this, we need to develop a balanced approach to worship. We need an approach that is holistic, that is, it takes into account all the biblical data and applies it to all of life.

To this end this study is set forth, not as an exhaustive exposition of all there is to know about worship, but as an exposition of the basic principles of biblical worship.

Chapter One
Worship Is All of Life

One of the greatest devices of Satan by which he has deceived multitudes of the people of God and thereby robbed them of their spiritual birthright is the secular/sacred dichotomy.

This dichotomy, which developed out of pagan Greek philosophy, has divided life into secular and sacred compartments. Actions, ideas and institutions are classified as being either "sacred" or "secular."

With this dichotomy in mind, the world tells us that religion is only one slice out of the whole pie of life. Our sacred actions and ideas should be restricted to church on Sunday. We are told, "You must not bring your religious convictions or ideas into the secular world of business, education or politics. Your religion is a private matter and does not belong to your public life in the secular world."

The world has always been irritated with Christians who have not bought the myth of the secular/sacred dichotomy. These believers see all of life as religious because the Bible says, "The earth is the Lord's, and all it contains, the world, and those who dwell in it" (Psalms 24:1).

The psalmist believed that every square inch

of this universe and all of life belong to God. There is no neutral or secular area of life. Every act of obedience to God in thought, word or deed is worship. As the apostle Paul stated to the Corinthians, "Whether, then, you eat or drink or whatever you do, do all to the glory of God" (1 Corinthians 10:31). To the Colossians, Paul said, "Whatever you do in word or deed do all in the name of the Lord Jesus, giving thanks through Him to God the Father" (Colossians 3:17). This is why the apostle Peter told his audience that they must live their lives in such a way "that in all things God may be glorified through Jesus Christ" (1 Peter 4:11).

In this light, Christians must realize that they cannot relegate or isolate worship to the 11:00 A.M. hour on Sundays. We are to live a life of worship 24 hours a day, seven days a week. Our entire life with all of its activities brings either glory or disgrace to the God we love.

Now, let it not be assumed that we are referring simply to doing certain religious activities frequently throughout the day. What we are saying is that the normal everyday activities which the world calls secular are actually ways of worshiping God. Such things as brushing teeth, sleeping, digging a ditch, programming a computer, cleaning a house, washing dishes, bowling or walking a dog are just as much worship as praying or singing a hymn. They are passive, unconscious acts of worship as opposed to active, conscious acts of worship. Thus we cannot limit worship to a few sacred activities.

Everything from work to food is worship if done to the glory of God.

It was this holistic view of worship that inspired the Protestant Reformers to reject the secular/sacred division. Luther thundered that the Christian who dug ditches was just as holy in his work as a priest was in his.

We should also point out that the reformational position that all work is holy means we must reject the separation between having a secular job and entering full-time Christian work. Anyone who talks in such terms reveals his or her unconscious commitment to the secular/sacred dichotomy.

The truth is that *all* work is full-time Christian work because whatever a Spirit-filled Christian does is holy and sacred. In this way the dignity of all work is upheld. Therefore, a Christian who works in the factory should have a sense of the dignity of his work, for it is holy and a way of worshiping the true God.

The reason why the Reformers rejected the secular/sacred dichotomy was that the Scriptures clearly taught that all believers are priests and ministers.

In Isaiah 61:1-9, the coming of the Messiah would "bring good news to the afflicted." He would "bind up the brokenhearted, proclaim liberty to captives, and freedom to prisoners" (v. 1). The result of His work was that all the people of God would become "priests of the Lord" and "ministers of our God" (v. 6).

The prophecy of Isaiah was fulfilled by the

Lord Jesus. As John tells us, He "loves us, and released us from our sins by His blood, and He has made us to be a kingdom, priests to His God and Father" (Revelation 1:5-6).

Peter also clearly taught the universal priesthood of the believer in 1 Peter 2:5, 9: "You also, as living stones, are being built up as a spiritual house for a holy priesthood, to offer up spiritual sacrifices acceptable to God through Jesus Christ. . . . But you are a chosen race, a royal priesthood."

Because all believers are priests, all work is priestly, holy and sacred. All believers can view their job as a holy service of worship to God. Paul even told lowly slaves to view themselves as the "slaves of Christ, doing the will of God from [your] heart." He said, "with good will render service, wholeheartedly, as to the Lord, and not to man" (Ephesians 6:6-7).

With the knowledge that we are priests of the Most High God and that whatever job we have is holy before God and a way of worship, this should make us realize that God is more concerned with what we are in terms of our character than what we do. For our worship to be acceptable to God we must be godly men and women. Note what the Scriptures say:

> But know that the Lord has set
> apart the godly man for Himself;
> The Lord hears when I call to Him
> *(Psalm 4:3).*

Therefore, let everyone who is
godly pray to Thee in a time when Thou
mayest be found; Surely in a flood of great
waters they shall not reach him
(Psalm 32:6).

But the prayer of the upright is His
delight *(Proverbs 15:8b).*

But He hears the prayer of
the righteous *(Proverbs 15:29b).*

What is godliness? Biblical godliness is that
consistent, habitual, careful and cautious piety
that concerns itself with living in harmony with
God and man and avoiding anything which de-
stroys that harmony.

How can we know if we are godly? Godliness
is evidenced in the life by certain clear signs:
- Prayerfulness *(Luke 18:1)*
- Christ-centeredness *(1 Corinthians 2:2)*
- Self-discipline *(1 Timothy 4:7)*
- Profitability in all things *(1 Timothy 4:8a)*
- Optimism in this life and in the life to come *(1 Timothy 4:8)*
- The embracing of doctrines that promote holiness *(1 Timothy 6:3; Titus 1:1)*
- Contentment *(1 Timothy 6:6)*
- Freedom from the love of money *(1 Timothy 6:7-10)*
- Greater concern for building character than for earning money *(1 Timothy 6:11-16)*

- Growth in graces and virtues *(2 Peter 1:3-8)*
- The keeping of eternity in view *(2 Peter 3: 11-12)*

By maintaining proper attitudes throughout the day, obeying the law of Christ in all of life, and by reacting to trials and problems by the power of the Spirit, a Christian can bring great glory and praise to God. Even unbelievers are forced to glorify God when they see a godly life. "Let your light shine before men in such a way that they may see your good works, and glorify your Father who is in heaven" (Matthew 5:16).

An ungodly person may pray, sing and go through all the activities which look like worship while God rejects everything he or she does. His or her character negates what he or she does.

If I regard wickedness in my heart,
the Lord will not hear *(Psalm 66:18)*.

The sacrifice of the wicked is
an abomination to the Lord,
(Proverbs 15:8a).

The Lord is far from the wicked
(Proverbs 15:29a).

He who turns away his ear
from listening to the law,
even his prayer is an abomination
(Proverbs 28:9).

Then some Pharisees and scribes came to Jesus from Jerusalem, saying, "Why do Your disciples transgress the tradition of the elders? For they do not wash their hands when they eat bread." And He answered and said to them, "And why do you yourselves transgress the commandment of God for the sake of your tradition? For God said, 'Honor your father and mother,' and, 'He who speaks evil of father or mother, let him be put to death.' But you say, 'Whoever shall say to his father or mother, "Anything of mine you might have been helped by has been given to God," he is not to honor his father or his mother.' And thus you invalidated the word of God for the sake of your tradition. You hypocrites, rightly did Isaiah prophesy of you, saying, 'This people honors Me with their lips, But their heart is far away from Me. But in vain do they worship Me, teaching as their doctrines the precepts of men' " *(Matthew 15:1-9).*

What is ungodliness? Ungodliness is practical atheism. It is selfish living with no concern for God, His will or Word (2 Corinthians 5:15). It is not that we consciously reject God or even the thought of God, but we live from day to day without any concern for or fear of God (Romans 3:18).

How can we tell if we are ungodly? Just as

there are signs in the life which reveal godliness, there are signs which evidence ungodliness. (See for example, 2 Timothy 3:1-5; 1 Timothy 4:1-3.) Some of these are:

- Self-love
- Love of money
- Boastfulness
- Arrogance
- The reviling of others
- Disobedience (disrespect) to those over you
- Ingratitude
- Unholiness
- Irreconcilability
- Lack of love
- Malicious gossip
- Lack of self-control
- Brutality
- Hatred of good
- Treachery
- Conceit
- A love of pleasure rather than a love of God
- Recklessness
- Only a "form" of godliness while denying the "power" in godliness
- False doctrine

Our character determines our worship. What we are is more foundational and crucial than what we do. Our person is more important than our performance. The failure to grasp these truths will result in much "wasted" worship, which is rejected by God Himself.

Worship as all of life is the foundation upon which private, family and public worship rests. To the degree that we are godly in our overall daily character, to that degree we will be effectual in private, family and public worship.

The real reason why so many professing Christians fail to enter into public worship, lead their families in worship or maintain their own private worship is that they are basically without God in their everyday character.

With this realization, it becomes clear why all the work to enliven worship services or establish family worship often fails. As long as we are dealing with basically ungodly people who do not really thirst or hunger after righteousness, we will never force them to have effectual worship in the church or home.

The following diagram reveals how seeing all of life as worship is foundational to the rest of worship:

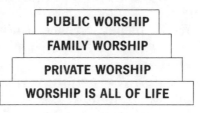

With this diagram in mind, let the reader ask himself or herself, "Am I a godly person? Do I desire to worship God as He has commanded us in His Word? Do I view myself as a priest and minister? Is all of my life worship and my occupation holy unto God?"

Chapter Two
My Private Worship of God

Having seen that all of life is worship, we need to focus our attention on the specific times and acts of worship during the day when we consciously worship God.

Every day is made holy to the Lord as we automatically and naturally pray, sing and praise God throughout the day. Just as the smoke of the sacrifices at the Temple ascended to God throughout the day, even so praise should ascend to God from our hearts throughout the day.

This has to do with developing the godly habit of responding to all events and issues in life by turning to God in praise or for deliverance.

When anything good happens to us, we should automatically say "Thank you Lord" for "every good thing bestowed and every perfect gift is from above" (James 1:17). Indeed, giving thanks to God is a duty as well as a privilege according to the Scriptures (Psalm 147:7; cf. Colossians 3:15).

God is greatly offended when His people neglect to thank Him for all His blessings because unthankfulness, according to Romans 1:21, is really *unbelief.*

The apostle Paul is a wonderful illustration of someone who developed the character quality of thankfulness. This Christlike quality in his life expressed itself in continual acts of thanksgiving. In Paul's epistles, we find at least 29 instances where he mentioned that he thanked God for specific people and things.

What about the evil things which come our way? How should we respond when the dinner burns, the car breaks down, we get sick or lose our jobs? Here, also, the godly habit and character quality of thankfulness should dominate our life.

Job said, " 'You speak as one of the foolish women speaks. Shall we indeed accept good from God and not accept adversity?' In all this Job did not sin with his lips" (Job 2:10). Job responded by worshiping God and saying " 'Naked I came from my mother's womb, and naked I shall return there. The Lord gave and the Lord has taken away. Blessed be the name of the Lord.' Through all this Job did not sin nor did he blame God" (Job 1:20-22).

When we respond to painful events, actions, people or things with bitterness, cursing, anger or a complaining spirit, we are not worshiping God as Job did. This is why the Scriptures command us not to respond in such negative ways but rather to develop the godly habit and character quality of thankfulness for the evil as well as the good which comes our way (see Ephesians 4:31-32; Colossians 3:8, 12-17).

We are told, "In everything give thanks; for

this is God's will for you in Christ Jesus" (1 Thessalonians 5:18). Regardless of what kind of situation we find ourselves in, we should give thanks to God for this is His will for us.

We are also told to "Always give thanks for all things in the name of our Lord Jesus Christ to God, even the Father" (Ephesians 5:20). We should give thanks *for* all things as well as *in* all things. There is no situation where a murmuring, complaining, bitter spirit is proper or acceptable. God always provides a way to escape from responding in such negative ways (1 Corinthians 10:13).

But we must ask, "On what grounds does God in Scripture command us to give thanks for the evil as well as for the good?" The answer lies in the doctrine of God's personal sovereignty over the lives of His people.

"And we know that God causes all things to work together for good to those who love God, who are called according to His purpose" (Romans 8:28). In this verse, we have God's guarantee that *everything* that happens to us in this life will ultimately work for our good.

This means that our failures as well as our victories are under God's personal sovereign control. Our sins become stepping stones toward holiness. God turns all our lemons into lemonade.

To be sure, this does not mean that we should think lightly of sin or of failure. What it does mean is that faith in God's personal sovereign control enables us to mine much gold out of the black pits in our lives. By faith we can build a castle out of the ashes. We can pick ourselves up, having learned humility and other lessons, and keep going forward in the Christian life. While we will fail, we can never be a failure, "if God is for us, who is against us? . . . But in all these things we overwhelmingly conquer through Him who loved us" (Romans 8:31, 37).

Joseph experienced many evil things at the hands of his brothers. His brothers were responsible for these evil things. Joseph pointed this out to them (Genesis 50:20). His brothers knew they were responsible.

> When Joseph's brothers saw that their father was dead, they said, "What if Joseph should bear a grudge against us and pay us back in full for all the wrong which we did to him!" So they sent a message to Joseph, saying, "Your father charged before he died saying, 'Thus you shall say to Joseph, "Please forgive, I beg you, the transgression of your brothers and their sin, for they did you wrong." ' And now, please forgive the transgression of the servants of the God of your father." And Joseph wept when they spoke to him *(Genesis 50:15-17)*.

Joseph responded in a godly way to the evil things his brothers did to him. Instead of bitterness and anger, we find Joseph thankful because he believed in God's personal sovereign control over all the evil his brothers did.

Then Joseph said to his brothers, "Please come closer to me." And they came closer. And he said, "I am your brother Joseph, whom you sold into Egypt. And now do not be grieved or angry with yourselves, because you sold me here; for God sent me before you to preserve life. For the famine has been in the land these two years, and there are still five years in which there will be neither plowing nor harvesting. And God sent me before you to preserve for you a remnant in the earth, and to keep you alive by a great deliverance. Now, therefore, it was not you who sent me here, but God; and He has made me a father to Pharaoh and lord of all his household and ruler over all the land of Egypt. Hurry and go up to my father, and say to him, 'Thus says your son Joseph, "God has made me lord of all Egypt; come down to me, do not delay. And you shall live in the land of Goshen, and you shall be near me, you and your children and your children's children and your flocks and your herds and all that you have. There I will also provide for you, for there are still five years of famine to come, lest you and your household and all that you have be impoverished." ' And behold, your eyes see, and the eyes of my brother Benjamin see, that it is my mouth which is speaking to you. Now you must tell my father of all my splendor in Egypt, and all that you have seen; and you must hurry and bring my father down here." Then he fell on his brother Benjamin's neck and wept; and Benjamin wept on his neck. And he kissed all his brothers and wept on them, and afterward his brothers talked with him *(Genesis 45:4-15)*.

"And as for you, you meant evil against me, but God meant it for good in order to bring about this present result, to preserve many people alive. So therefore, do not be afraid; I will provide for you and your little ones." So he comforted them and spoke kindly to them *(Genesis 50:20-21)*.

The response of Joseph revealed that he had an unshakable faith in "Him who works all things after the counsel of His will" (Ephesians 1:11). Joseph thanked God *for* and *in* all things.

There is a poem which has helped me in my darkest hours. It is called "The Weaver."

> My life is but a weaving
> Between my Lord and me;
> I cannot choose the colors,
> He worketh steadily:
> Often times He chooseth sorrow,
> And I in foolish pride;
> Forget He sees the upper,
> And I the underside.
> The dark threads are as needful
> In the Weaver's skillful hand;
> As the threads of gold and silver
> In the pattern He has planned.

Not till the loom is silent
And the shuttle cease to fly,
Shall God unroll the canvas
And explain the reason why.

To this we add,

God would not send the darkness
If He felt we could bear the light;
We would not cling to His guiding hand,
If the way were always bright.
So, He sends the blinding darkness
And the furnace's sevenfold heat;
'Tis the only way, believe me,
To keep you close to the Master's feet.

By developing the godly habit and character quality of thankfulness and learning how to respond in a positive manner to everything which comes our way, the whole of our lives becomes an orchestra of praise to the God who rules on high.

While unscheduled private worship should be ascending to God throughout the day, the child of God should set apart a definite time during the day when he can give himself totally to worship.

The biblical examples of believers who set apart specific and definite times to worship God every day should stir us to follow their practice as well as their beliefs.

David said: "In the morning, O Lord, Thou wilt hear my voice; in the morning I will order my prayer to Thee and eagerly watch" (Psalm

5:3). Later David stated in a fuller way, "Seven times a day I praise Thee, because of Thy righteous ordinances" (Psalm 119:164).

The practice of private worship was so ingrained into Daniel's character that even in the face of death, he maintained his times of worship.

> All the commissioners of the kingdom, the prefects and the satraps, the high officials and the governors have consulted together that the king should establish a statute and enforce an injunction that anyone who makes a petition to any god or man besides you, O king, for thirty days, shall be cast into the lions' den. Now, O king, establish the injunction and sign the document so that it may not be changed, according to the law of the Medes and Persians, which may not be revoked. Therefore King Darius signed the document, that is, the injunction. Now when Daniel knew that the document was signed, he entered his house (now in his roof chamber he had windows open toward Jerusalem); and he continued kneeling on his knees three times a day, praying and giving thanks before his God, as he had been doing previously *(Daniel 6:7-10)*.

Even our Lord Himself set apart time for private worship (see Mark 1:35).

These examples are sufficient to show any Spirit-filled Christian the path of obedience and blessing. Regardless of whether it is at the beginning of the day (Psalm 5:3) or at the end of the day (Psalm 63:5-6) we should have a definite time each day when we give ourselves to concentrated worship.

What should we do in private worship? Begin by praying for the filling of the Spirit (Luke 11:13). Why? The Spirit is called "the Spirit of grace and supplication" (Zechariah 12:10) because all true worship comes from Him. True spiritual worship begins and ends with God Himself. Thus our worship must be dependent on the Spirit, not on the flesh (Philippians 3:3).

We need to keep in mind what prayer is. Prayer is a sincere, heartfelt outpouring of our souls to God through Christ by the Spirit to present praise, thanksgiving, our needs or the needs of others.

Our physical position in prayer is a matter of Christian liberty. We may pray standing, walking, sitting, kneeling or lying prostrate on the ground with our faces to the floor. This last is physically the most humbling and submissive before God. If the reader has not worshiped God while lying prostrate before Him, he or she should try this biblical position.

In our private worship, there should be singing or chanting unto the Lord. Singing unto God is such a normal and vital part of worship that the apostle Paul refers to it as one of the first signs of the filling of the Spirit (Ephesians 5:19). We are urged to sing unto God by command or example no less than 75 times in the

Scriptures! The singing is clearly not just mental but also vocal—aloud. Even the monotone should chant praise to God! Singing aloud prepares the heart within.

Worship should include the reading of and meditating on the Scriptures. As we read Scripture, we should always ask ourselves these questions:

- Is there a doctrine to believe?
- Is there a command to obey?
- Is there a promise to claim?
- Is there a threat to heed?
- Is there a praise to offer?

When meditating on Scripture, there are five things which we can do to make the passage "come alive":

1. We should read the passage aloud. In this way we are using the ear gate as well as the eye gate. Many have also found that reading Scripture aloud prevents the mind from wandering.

2. We should then reread the passage aloud, but this time make it apply to us personally if possible. For example, a personalized John 3:16 would read,

> For God so loved *me* that He gave
> His only Son that if *I* would believe
> in Him, *I* would not perish but have
> everlasting life.

3. We should close our eyes and try to visualize a picture that illustrates what the passage is saying. For example, when meditating on

Psalm 1, we can visualize a tree planted by a river and the chaff of the wheat being blown away by the wind.

4. We might chant or sing the passage. The early church practiced writing and singing songs of praise. They would bring their songs to church and share them with the Body (see 1 Corinthians 14:26).

5. We should "activize" the passage—that is, put into action any commands which apply to us. When we read, "Sing unto God" in Psalm 68:4, we should stop and sing. When we read, "Humble yourself in the sight of the Lord" (James 4:9), we should fall on our faces before God and humble ourselves by confessing that we are nothing and He is everything. We should confess that the only thing we can claim as our own is our sin. All goodness comes from God.

We must remember that the mere reading and believing of a command in Scripture is not sufficient to please God. We must go on to obey what we read.

There are times when we should fast as part of our private worship (see Matthew 6:16-18). What is fasting? Fasting is the deliberate foregoing of food, or food and water. It can last for an hour, a day or weeks.

Fasting, in and of itself, does not merit God's grace. It is an empty work. It is what we do while fasting that determines whether or not we receive God's grace.

While fasting, we are to spend our time praying, singing, reading Scripture. The mere foregoing of food without such things as prayer is dieting, not fasting.

In the Old Testament, individuals, churches and entire nations fasted (see Psalm 35:13; Nehemiah 9:1; Jonah 3:4-10). The New Testament records that Jesus, the apostles and the early church fasted (Matthew 4:2; Acts 13:2-3; 14:23). Jesus clearly assumed that just as His disciples would pray and give offerings to God, they would fast as well. Thus He gave instruction concerning fasting (Matthew 6:16-18). He prophesied that fasting would characterize His people after He ascended to heaven (Matthew 9:14-15).

Why should we fast? The general purpose of fasting is to increase our spiritual awareness in order to discern God's Word and will for some issue that has arisen. It is the giving of total, undivided concentration and attention to spiritual issues.

What specific issues have prompted believers to fast?

1. They have fasted in order to discern God's will in a specific matter (Judges 20:26; Acts 13: 2-3).

2. They have fasted in repentance for sin (Nehemiah 9:1; 1 Samuel 7:6; 2 Samuel 12:16-22).

3. They have fasted out of concern for the work of God when it is failing (Nehemiah 1:4).

4. They have fasted to gain spiritual alertness to overcome satanic temptations and attacks (Matthew 4:2).

5. They have fasted for deliverance from enemies (2 Chronicles 20:3; Ezra 8:21-23).

6. They have fasted in order to humble themselves before God (Psalm 69:10-11, 13).

7. They have fasted to give themselves to special times of worship and praise (Luke 2:37; Acts 13:2-3).

8. They have fasted when calamities befell them or others (1 Samuel 31:13; 2 Samuel 12:16).

9. They have fasted to exorcise stubborn demons (Matthew 17:21; Mark 9:29).

10. They have fasted before choosing church leaders (Acts 14:23).

Total fasting should not be attempted by those who medically need to ingest food frequently. But these individuals can nibble cheese or nuts during the fast without substantially interrupting their concentration on God.

As we begin fasting as part of our private worship, we need to keep in mind the rules set forth by Jesus:

> And whenever you fast, do not put on a gloomy face as the hypocrites do, for they neglect their appearance in order to be seen fasting by men. Truly I say to you, they have their reward in full. But you, when you fast, anoint your head, and wash your face so that you may not be seen fasting by men, but by your Father who is in secret; and your Father who sees in secret will repay you *(Matthew 6:16-18).*

In our worship we should offer special thanksgiving for all the blessings of God. Such psalms as Psalm 103 should be used to direct our thanksgiving.

We should also adore, magnify and exalt the Lord (Luke 1:46; Psalm 118:28). To magnify or exalt the Lord means to ascribe unto the Lord all the glory due to His name or character (Psalm 29:1-2). To exalt the Lord means that we tell Him that He is great and glorious and merciful, that He alone is God, the Creator and Sustainer of the universe. It is to praise Him, to magnify and lift up His name. It is to love Him because He first loved us.

In these ways God can be worshiped in private. This worship should naturally flow out of our hearts, in gratitude for all that God has done for and in us. Indeed, private worship is the natural product of a godly life. It is one of the fruits of the filling of the Spirit. And where the Spirit is, there is liberty (2 Corinthians 3:17).

To the degree we worship God in private, to that degree we will worship God with our families and at church. To the degree we enter into, enjoy and express ourselves freely in private worship, to that degree we will be able to enter into, enjoy and express ourselves freely in family and public worship. Therefore, if we desire to maintain and enjoy family worship and public worship, we must maintain and enjoy private worship.

Will you commit yourself to private worship?

Suggested Readings

Bounds, Edward M. *Power Through Prayer.* Chicago: Moody Press, 1979.

Bunyan, J. *Prayer.* Jenkintown, Pa: Sovereign Grace, _____.

Calvin, John. *Devotions and Prayers of John Calvin.* Grand Rapids: Baker, 1979.

Henry, Matthew. *The Secret of Communion with God.* New Canaan, Conn.: Keats Publishing, 1980.

Watson, Thomas. *A Divine Cordial.* Alexandria, La.: Lamplighter Publications, 1979.

Chapter Three
Worship at the Family Level

Once we begin to view all of life as worship, we will naturally desire that our families will worship God with us throughout the day and at least together once a day. This is true because family worship is the overflow of a life of worship. It is the inevitable consequence of the Spirit-filled life of a dedicated Christian. But is family worship a *necessity* or a *luxury*?

The Scriptures assert the necessity of family worship. Family worship is set forth as something that the family does together throughout the day. Each Christian home is to be a house of praise and worship unto God every day.

In the first sense, family worship is based on a spontaneous and natural worship of God throughout the day. Family worship, therefore, cannot be restricted to a devotional period at night but must encompass the entire day.

One of the greatest challenges parents face is the creating of a theistic environment for their children. Children must be trained to see all of life as related to God. They must be trained in a theistic world and life view where there is no secular/sacred division.

God commanded His people to develop a theistic environment for their children.

> Hear, O Israel! The Lord is our God, the
> Lord is one! And you shall love the Lord
> your God with all your heart and with all
> your soul and with all your might. And
> these words, which I am commanding you
> today, shall be on your heart; and you shall
> teach them diligently to your sons and
> shall talk of them when you sit in your
> house and when you walk by the way and
> when you lie down and when you rise up
> *(Deuteronomy 6:4-7).*

Notice that Moses is not speaking concerning a
family altar at night but the creating of a theistic environment for the children in which they
are instructed about God throughout the day.

Christian homes should be places of worship
where the entire family is trained to consciously
"live and move and have [their] being in God"
(Acts 17:28, KJV). We should point out the glory
of God in the beautiful sunsets. The handiwork
of God in creating the smallest flower should be
celebrated by the whole family. All of life should
be rooted and grounded in God.

Throughout the day, worship should be
ascending to God from united family members.
It should be as natural as breathing for our
families to burst into spontaneous songs of
praise to God during the day.

Christian music should be a constant part of
everyday life in a Christian home in order to
create a theistic and godly atmosphere. The

following acrostic from the word MUSIC brings out the importance of Christian music in the home.

Music creates a godly atmosphere in the home,
Unifies the family's feelings and fellowship,
Stresses scriptural truths for the family,
Inspires the family to action and participation,
Channels the family's thoughts Godward.

When professing Christian parents allow ungodly music to be played in the home and then find their children developing ungodly attitudes toward the Lord and the family, the root cause is apparent. Ungodly music produces an ungodly atmosphere. It will result in tragedy.

Praying as a family is another area which must mark the entire day. Family members should go to prayer together when any member is sick or has a problem. Every time they get into the car, the family should pray for protection and a successful trip. When a family trial comes, the family should set apart days of fasting and prayer together.

Informal times of gathering around the piano and praising God in songs of worship will enrich family life. Giving thanks to God for deliverance, healing, answered prayer and all blessings received should be as natural for the family as saying grace at meals.

It is also helpful to place Scripture texts on the walls of the home. Children should grow up surrounded by God's Word.

The foundation of family worship is the viewing of all of family life as worship. If a family goes through the mere ritual of a family altar at night, but the rest of their family life is secular, that is, devoid of praise, worship, singing, praying, celebrating, that family is guilty of gross hypocrisy. The children will not be fooled. They will know that their parents do not have a real heart for God. The parents' religion is relegated to special times and does not apply to all of life.

It is of utmost importance that we commit ourselves to worshiping God with our families throughout the day. It is essential that we dedicate ourselves to creating a godly environment in our homes. Joshua's example should serve as our pattern. He said, "But as for me and my house, we will serve [worship] the Lord" (Joshua 24:15).

Once our families develop the habit of worshiping God together throughout the day, we will not find opposition to establishing a family altar—a specific time each day when the family gathers for worship. The degree of ungodliness in the atmosphere of the home determines the degree of opposition to a family altar.

That the family should gather to worship the Lord together is clearly the teaching of Scripture:

> Sing to the Lord, all the earth; proclaim good tidings of His salvation from day to day. Tell of His glory among the nations,

His wonderful deeds among all the peoples. For great is the Lord, and greatly to be praised; He also is to be feared above all gods. For all the gods of the peoples are idols, but the Lord made the heavens. Splendor and majesty are before Him, strength and joy are in His place. Ascribe to the Lord, O families of the peoples, ascribe to the Lord glory and strength. Ascribe to the Lord the glory due His name *(1 Chronicles 16:23-29)*.

The prophet Jeremiah calls down God's anger upon families who neglect to worship:

Pour out Thy wrath on the nations that do not know Thee, and on the families that do not call Thy name; for they have devoured Jacob; they have devoured him and consumed him, and have laid waste his habitation *(Jeremiah 10:25)*.

God's curse falls upon the families that do not worship Him. The passage above explains why so many evangelical homes produce ungodly rebels. Some parents do not lead the family in worship and the curse of God will fall upon them.

It is also clear that the father bears the main responsibility to lead the family in worship.

And, fathers, do not provoke your children to anger; but bring them up in the discipline and instruction of the Lord *(Ephesians 6:4)*.

The father stands as the high priest of his

family (see, for instance, Genesis 49:2, 28; 2 Samuel 6:20). He will bless or curse his family. The New Testament also emphasizes the importance of the father taking the spiritual leadership in the family (see Acts 11:14; 16: 31-34; 18:8; John 4:53).

What if the father is unconverted or unwilling or unable to lead the family? First, his responsibility as the spiritual head of the family is a *fact* whether or not he is converted or willing. On the day of judgment, he will be held responsible for such leadership. Second, to be a man as God intended him to be, he must lead his family in worship.

If all this fails, the wife must seek her husband's permission to lead the family until such time as he is prepared to do so. It must be emphasized that she is leading with a view to her husband's eventually doing so.

Many fathers do not lead in devotional exercises because they are semi-illiterate. Their pride would be wounded if they stumbled, trying to read the Bible in front of their children who read better than they.

Some fathers do not lead the family for fear of failure. They do not know what to do and are too proud to ask for help. They feel embarrassed and ignorant. So, they resist leading the family even though they know it is right to do so.

All these kinds of problems can be overcome by creative alternatives. The father can appoint someone else to read instead of reading himself. If he cannot sing, his wife can lead in song at his direction. His oversight is what determines his leadership. It does not matter if tapes of the Scriptures are played as long as the father is overseeing the worship time.

The time of day in which to worship is always a problem. It should be when the entire family is gathered. This is usually only at the evening meal. In homes where a family member works the night shift, the family may eat together at breakfast or lunch.

Regardless of the time, there must be a specific time every day when the family worships God together. We tend to forget that the "breaking of bread" and the worshiping of God were often done in the context of the home (Acts 2:46). Here is where the father bears the chief responsibility. Even though it is increasingly difficult to compete with TV, school activities and other demands, the father must see to it that his family worships together every day.

What should we do in family worship? The main thing is to worship God in creative ways which cause the entire family to participate.

The family should sing lively hymns, songs, psalms, choruses, rounds, action songs, prayer songs, children's songs. They might practice making up songs to praise God for what He did for them that day.

To encourage singing in worship, we parents should stress musical training for our children. If there is any talent for the playing of musical instruments, this talent should be trained and then used during family worship. If every child played a different instrument, this could aid in worship.

The reading of Scripture, the explaining of the passage and the answering of questions from the passage should always be a part of worship. The attention should be on truths to believe and character qualities to develop.

One way to sharpen a Scripture reading is to act out the passage. For example, the resurrection of Jairus's daughter could be a family play performed in the home. The smallest child could be the daughter and the rest of the family could be Jesus, Jairus, the crowd of mourners, etc. Acting out scriptural plays as a family makes Scripture come alive to everyone. After a drama has been perfected, it might be put on for the Sunday school or church. The excitement of ministering to others as a byproduct of family worship will conquer even apathetic teenagers.

There should also be a time for each family member to tell what happened that day and to give reasons why he or she wants to praise God for those things. Even the smallest child will have something to say.

If all Christian homes practiced the giving of verbal praise to God in the home, when it came to testimony meetings in the church, they would be trained to speak up for God. The reason why the pastor must drag out testimonies like a dentist pulling teeth is that his people do not testify in the home. If they are too proud and too embarrassed to testify at home, they will sit in church with a closed mouth.

Prayer is, of course, a vital part of family worship. But it is prayer as it relates to the personal needs of the family. One child may want prayer for a test coming in school. The mother may be sick. The father may be struggling with bills. As God answers these prayers, it should be reported back to the family. One of the greatest heritages we can give our children is the firm conviction that God answers prayer.

With younger children, handicrafts can also play a part in family worship. The story of Noah and the flood can be visualized by making Noah, his family, the ark and the animals out of Play-Doh or clay. Another idea might be to make cookies by following the directions in the cookbook. Then make some other cookies putting in whatever ingredients the children want to add. When we follow the cookbook the cookies are good. But when we pour in as much salt as we please, or do whatever we want, the cookies are inedible. In the same way, we will spoil our lives unless we live according to God's directions for happy living as given in His Word.

Games can also be used. There are many exciting Christian games on the market that will bring joy and delight. One game in particular is the Character Clues game from the Institute in Basic Youth Conflicts. It is a card game where the participants must memorize godly character qualities and their definitions. Learning can be fun and games can be used by wise parents to instruct their children.

There may be times when a trial or calamity

strikes the family. That is an appropriate time to proclaim a family fast. Instead of preparing and eating a meal, the family spends time praying and singing before God. When children see that their parents are so concerned about something that they proclaim a fast, they will know that their parents are genuine Christians sold out to Christ Jesus. These children will not grow up rebelling against the hypocrisy of parents who play at religion for they will *know* that their parents are real.

To get started in family worship is sometimes harder than anything else. The fear of failure aided by pride prevents many parents from even trying.

Just how can family worship be started?

First, we must work on worshiping God in all of life.

Second, we must practice private worship. Although family worship rests upon our own private worship, family worship can never be substituted for private worship.

Third, we must humble ourselves before God and others. Perhaps the pastor or church elders could help. They will usually be glad to come to the house and show a church family what to do.

Fourth, the Christian education department or committee in the church might be asked to set up a program to help families get started.

Fifth, the books recommended at the close of this chapter are designed to help parents set up or maintain good family worship.

Sixth, we must seek the filling of the Spirit, for

without His assistance family worship will be in vain.

There is a problem today with the Sunday school supplanting the father's role in the religious education of his family and even family worship itself.

The subject of the religious education of children is a growing area of concern. The reason why there is a growing concern over the relationship between the family and the Sunday school is because it appears that the family has relinquished its God-given responsibilities to the Sunday school (which it cannot really do). Christian families do not worship together, and parents do not teach their own children at home because they assume that this is the purpose or function of the Sunday school.

The following diagram illustrates the absolute antithesis between the traditional concept of Sunday school and the scriptural responsibilities of parents.

The Religious Education of Children

QUESTION	TRADITION	SCRIPTURE
1. Who is responsible for it?	Sunday school teachers	The parents (Ephesians 6:4)
2. Where is it to be done?	At the church building	In the home and everywhere (Deuteronomy 6:4-9)

QUESTION	TRADITION	SCRIPTURE
3. When is it to be done?	Sunday, 9:30 A.M., once a week	Every day, all day and at specific times of family worship (Deuteronomy 6:4-9)
4. Who has oversight?	Sunday school superintendent or teacher, pastor, board	The father (Ephesians 6:4)
5. Who is to "blame" if the children grow up rebels?	The Sunday school, church, pastor	The parents (1 Samuel 3:11-14)
6. What will be taught?	Bible stories, lessons	The whole counsel of God

Why do parents panic if they feel the Sunday school is not good enough? Why do churches split over Sunday school? Why has Sunday school generated so much bitterness and contention in churches?

Ironically, the very parents who panic the most over Sunday school are usually delinquent about family worship. They experience failure in trying to set up or maintain family worship. This produces guilt over their failure. Then their pride takes over and they refuse to face the failure or even to admit it. They experience panic about Sunday school because their children get nothing at home. Finally, their guilt drives them to blame the teachers, the superintendent or the pastor for not training their children right. They seek to relieve their own guilt by placing the blame on others. If their children grow up to become rebels, they blame the Sunday school instead of accepting the responsibility themselves.

People need to be aware that Sunday school is *not* a biblical institution. Neither God nor Christ ever established it. It did not develop until the last century. The parents fulfilled their responsibilities for their children personally, instead of pushing them onto the church.

The Sunday school can be redesigned to aid parents in family worship instead of working against them. When parents teach in Sunday school, they learn how to prepare and teach a lesson. This training is needed for family worship. Sunday school trains children to sit and learn from the Bible. They learn songs about God. All these things are an aid to family worship. The Sunday school can give take-home material that offers creative ideas for family worship during the week. It can actively support family worship by requesting families to role play their family worship before the congregation. The adult Sunday school can spend time in discussing family worship.

Ultimately, the people of God must be reeducated concerning the purpose of Sunday school. While family worship is the foundation, Sunday school is the capstone.

By restructuring the Sunday school to work for and with fathers in setting up and maintaining family worship, we can retain the Sunday school as a beneficial and practical institution even though it has no explicit biblical warrant. Its justification comes from the biblical principle, "Let all things be done for edification" (1 Corinthians 14:26).

What are the goals of family worship? The salvation of every member of the family is certainly the highest goal. The second goal is the growth in grace or sanctification of the Christians in the family. Family worship will also produce a godly atmosphere where the knowledge of God is a family concern and a family joy. Let it never be forgotten that just as "the family that prays together stays together," so "the family that worships together works together." Will your family begin the joy of family worship?

Suggested Reading

Schooland Marian, M. *Leading Little Ones to God*. Grand Rapids: Eerdmans, 1970.

Rogers, Jack and Sharee. *The Family Together*. Action House, 1976.

Richards, Lawrence. *A Theology of Church Leadership*. Grand Rapids: Zondervan, 1980.

————. *A New Face for the Church*. Grand Rapids: Zondervan, 1981.

"Weekly Bible Reader." *Family Scrapbook*. Austin: Bible Discovery Aids, 1979.

Zabel, Ted. *Family Scrapbook*. Camp Hill, Pa.: Christian Publications, 1981.

Chapter Four
Public Worship: the Worshiper

Having examined the nature and purpose of worshiping God in private and with the family, we now come to the public worship of God in the gathered assembly of the saints.

What we do in church in order to worship God is crucial to our Christian life. A "high" Sunday in which the glory of God descends upon the congregation and it is carried to heaven on "eagles' wings" sets the tone for the entire week. How often have we gone to church feeling depressed and through the worship service we were set free to rejoice before Him? Our burdens were lifted and our spirits were liberated.

On the other hand, when we go to church joyful but the service is dull and the spirit of the other worshipers is down, our entire week can be depressed because of it. When God does not rend the heavens and come down to dwell in the midst of His people, it is a "low" Sunday. The heavens are as brass. Our spirits are shackled instead of liberated. Our burdens are not lifted but rather increased.

Now we complete the full circle of worship. Our private worship affects our family worship. Our family worship in turn affects our public worship. Our public worship affects our private worship which in turn, affects our family worship. All these aspects of worship relate to each other for all of life is worship. What we do in the public worship of God will directly affect what we do in the following week. The only way to live a life of worship is to give ourselves to private, family and public worship with all our hearts and souls and minds and strength. No aspect of worship can be dispensed with or viewed as non-essential.

With this in mind we now turn to an examination of the basic principles of public worship.

In public worship two different things occur. On the one hand, *internal* worship is taking place in the hearts of God's people. On the other hand, *external* worship is taking place verbally and visibly in the congregation. Thus our first basic principle of public worship is to make the distinction between internal and external worship. If we fail to grasp the difference between these two kinds of worship, our public worship will be hindered.

Internal worship refers to the inner attitudes of the heart and mind while engaged in worship. It refers to the subjective feelings in our hearts while worshiping. Internal worship has to do with our spirits and only we and God know if we are truly worshiping. Internal worship is not perceivable by the five senses and others cannot judge whether or not we are actually engaged in internal worship.

External worship refers to the outward acts of

worship which are composed of what we say or do while engaged in public worship. External worship *is* perceivable by the senses. Therefore others can see and judge what we are doing. It refers to the forms, liturgies, hymns, order of services, etc. which compose the visible and audible parts of public worship.

The second principle is that internal worship is the essence of true worship. In this sense it is more necessary and crucial than external worship. Internal worship has to do with the *essence* of worship while external worship refers to the *form* of worship.

The Scriptures are abundantly clear that God is more concerned with our attitudes while in worship than with what we say or do. God said to Samuel when he was seeking a king to replace Saul:

> "Do not look at his appearance or at the height of his stature, because I have rejected him; for God sees not as man sees, for man looks at the outward appearance, but the Lord looks at the heart" *(1 Samuel 16:7).*

Conscious that God is examining our hearts while we are engaged in worship, we must realize that our hearts are more important than our hands. Our minds are more important than the medium. Our attitudes are more important than our actions.

An overconcern with forms and ceremonies reveals an overemphasis on external worship.

The Pharisees and all other legalists reveal their true nature when seen in this light. An unyielding dogmatism which refuses to change any part of the worship service and which clings tenaciously to the traditions of men is indicative of the attitude of the Pharisees who opposed Christ in His day.

The emphasis therefore should be placed on internal worship instead of external worship. A church that prides itself because of its great theatrical entertainment is missing the mark. God could not care less if there are solos, duets or choir numbers if they are not a true manifestation of internal worship. After all, God is looking for true spiritual worship from the hearts of His people. He is not impressed with mere entertainment from the platform. And it is doubtful if we can "entertain" God or that He even desires us to do so. Worship is not to be entertainment-centered or man-centered but God-centered. Therefore the emphasis must be on the internal aspects of worship.

The third principle naturally flows out of the second principle. It is possible to be guilty of having the proper external worship without having the corresponding proper internal worship. This is what the Scriptures call "hypocritical worship." When our external worship does not correspond to what is really going on in our hearts, we are guilty of hypocritical worship.

Our Lord pointed out this problem in His own day:

And the Pharisees and some of the scribes gathered together around Him when they had come from Jerusalem, and had seen that some of His disciples were eating their bread with impure hands, that is, unwashed. (For the Pharisees and all the Jews do not eat unless they carefully wash their hands, thus observing the traditions of the elders; and when they come from the market place, they do not eat unless they cleanse themselves; and there are many other things which they have received in order to observe, such as the washing of cups and pitchers and copper pots.) And the Pharisees and the scribes asked Him, "Why do Your disciples not walk according to the tradition of the elders, but eat their bread with impure hands?" And He said to them, "Rightly did Isaiah prophesy of you hypocrites, as it is written, 'This people honors Me with their lips, but their heart is far away from Me. But in vain do they worship Me, teaching as doctrines the precepts of men.' Neglecting the commandment of God, you hold to the tradition of men." He was also saying to them, "You nicely set aside the commandment of God in order to keep your tradition. For Moses said, 'Honor your father and your mother'; and, 'He who speaks evil of father or mother, let him be put to death'; but you say, 'If a man says to his father or his mother, anything of mine you might have been helped by is Corban (that is to say, given to God),' you no longer permit him to do anything for his father or his mother; thus invalidating the word of God by your tradition which you have handed down; and you do many things such as that" *(Mark 7:1-13)*.

Christ was simply echoing the complaint God voiced to Isaiah:

Then the Lord said, "Because this people draw near with their words and honor Me with their lip service, but they remove their hearts far from Me, and their reverence for Me consists of tradition learned by rote, therefore behold, I will once again deal marvelously with this people, wondrously marvelous; and the wisdom of their wise men shall perish, and the discernment of their discerning men shall be concealed" *(Isaiah 29:13-14)*.

God rejects our external worship when it is hypocritical:

Hear the word of the Lord, you rulers of Sodom; give ear to the instruction of our God, you people of Gomorrah. "What are your multiplied sacrifices to Me?" says the Lord. "I have had enough of burnt offerings of rams, and the fat of fed cattle. And I take no pleasure in the blood of bulls, lambs, or goats. When you come to appear before Me, who requires of you this trampling of My courts? Bring your worthless offerings no longer, their incense is an abomination to Me. New moon and sabbath, the calling of assemblies—I cannot endure iniquity and the solemn assembly. I hate your new moon festivals and your appointed feasts, they have become a burden to Me. I am weary of bearing them. So when you spread out your hands in prayer, I will hide My eyes from you, yes, even though you multiply prayers, I will not listen. Your hands are full of bloodshed" *(Isaiah 1:10-15).*

While we all agree that the Pharisees were hypocrites, we must ask ourselves some hard questions. Have we ever sung a hymn while our minds were blank or daydreaming or anxiously turning over some problem we faced? We sang the words of the hymn mechanically and took no notice of what they meant. We were thus guilty of hypocritical worship. God was not glorified. Nor were we edified. We honored God with our lips but our hearts were far from Him.

The author of Hebrews points out another example of hypocritical worship:

For this reason we must pay much closer attention to what we have heard, lest we drift away from it. For if the word spoken through angels proved unalterable, and every transgression and disobedience received a just recompense, how shall we escape if we neglect so great a salvation? After it was at the first spoken through the

Lord, it was confirmed to us by those who heard *(Hebrews 2:1-3).*

Have we ever been guilty of sitting through a sermon and, instead of listening and obeying God's Word, sleeping, daydreaming or worrying about something? We were guilty of hypocritical worship. God is worshiped when we listen to and obey His Word. Hearing a sermon is worship. But if we "hear" and do not "listen," we are guilty of hypocritical worship.

In these situations we can see the utter difference between the inner reality of what really goes on in our hearts and what is merely the following of external forms of worship. How God must be grieved when we treat Him so shabbily! God is not deceived by our hypocrisy.

While all of us must admit with sorrow that we fall into hypocritical worship at times, we must point out that a consistent life of hypocritical worship is the surest sign of an unregenerate heart (Mark 7:6-7; 2 Timothy 3:5).

If a person consistently tunes out the sermon and sits with glazed eyes and blank mind, he does not have any warrant to profess that he has been born again. The apostle John simply stated:

> And by this we know that we have come to know Him, if we keep His commandments. The one who says, "I have come to know Him," and does not keep His com-

mandments, is a liar, and the truth is not in him *(1 John 2:3-4)*.

This is why the author of Hebrews equated failure to listen to the Word of God with neglecting salvation (Hebrews 2:1, cf. 2:3). How shall we escape divine judgment if we neglect salvation by letting our minds wander during the sermon? This was the sobering application that the author of Hebrews placed on the consciences of his readers.

It is for this reason that the primary emphasis should be placed on making sure that we are really worshiping God in our hearts by our spirit instead of relying on external forms and ceremonies.

The fourth basic principle of public worship is to define carefully what constitutes truly acceptable internal worship before God.

What is internal worship? Of what does it consist?

Internal or heart worship must be understood in terms of a communion or fellowship which arises out of the interaction between a redeemed sinner and God while that redeemed sinner is contemplating God.

Perhaps we should begin by emphasizing that the worship must be communion or fellowship with God. It is a two-way street instead of a dead-end or a one-way street. God is blessing us as we bless Him. He is edifying us as we glorify Him. Worship which does not involve an interaction between God and man is like a bridge broken at either end. No true worship is possible.

The apostle John speaks of our worship in terms of communion when he says:

> What we have seen and heard we proclaim to you also, that you also may have fellowship with us; and indeed our fellowship is with the Father, and with His Son Jesus Christ *(1 John 1:3).*

To this the apostle Paul adds that the goal of effectual calling is to bring sinners into a fellowship relationship to Christ.

> God is faithful, through whom you were called into fellowship with His Son, Jesus Christ our Lord *(1 Corinthians 1:9).*

Paul also speaks of worship as the fellowship of the Spirit:

> The grace of the Lord Jesus Christ, and the love of God, and the fellowship of the Holy Spirit, be with you all *(2 Corinthians 13:14).*

In the light of these passages, we should be concerned to invoke God's blessing and to make sure that our worship is composed of listening and responding to God as well as of speaking to God.

> Hear my prayer, O Lord! And let my cry for help come to Thee. Do not hide Thy face from me in the day of my distress; incline

> Thine ear to me; in the day when I call answer me quickly *(Psalm 102:1-2)*.

> I will hear what God the Lord will say; for He will speak peace to His people, to His godly ones; but let them not turn back to folly *(Psalm 85:8)*.

> Cease striving and know that I am God; I will be exalted among the nations. I will be exalted in the earth *(Psalm 46:10)*.

One aspect of worship that has fallen into disuse is the biblical practice of invoking God's blessing before we render worship to Him.

Listen to the psalmist as he invokes God's blessing before he presents his prayers, cries, requests and worship:

> Answer me when I call, O God of my righteousness! . . . be gracious to me and hear my prayer *(Psalm 4:1)*.

> Give ear to my words, O Lord, consider my groaning. Heed the sound of my cry for help, my King and my God *(Psalm 5:1-2)*.

> Hear a just cause, O Lord, give heed to my cry; give ear to my prayer *(Psalm 17:1)*.

> Give ear to my prayer, O God; and do not hide Thyself from my supplication. Give heed to me, and answer me *(Psalm 55:1-2)*.

> Hear my cry, O God; give heed to my prayer *(Psalm 61:1)*.

> Incline Thine ear, O Lord, and answer me *(Psalm 86:1)*.

> Hear my prayer, O Lord! And let my cry for help come to Thee *(Psalm 102:1)*.

> Out of the depths I have cried to Thee, O Lord. Lord, hear my voice! Let Thine ears be attentive to the voice of my supplications *(Psalm 130:1-2)*.

> O Lord, I call upon Thee; hasten to me! Give ear to my voice when I call to Thee! May my prayer be counted as incense before Thee! The lifting up of my hands as the evening offering *(Psalm 141:1-2)*.

> Hear my prayer, O Lord, give ear to my supplications! Answer me in Thy faithfulness, in Thy righteousness! *(Psalm 143:1)*.

It is obvious from these verses that the psalmist invoked God's blessing before he worshiped. In contrast to his practice, too many modern evangelicals rush into God's presence without the least preparation. Could it be that they do this because they think worship consists of certain actions which *they* do while *God* is passive in worship?

To solve this problem, we must develop a dynamic concept of worship which magnifies the interaction between God and man in the communion or fellowship of worship. This concept should revolve around the central truth that true worship, rather than simply singing or talking "about" God is personally and individually "with" God and "to" God. Worship is communion.

If it is to be acceptable to God, where will internal worship take place? It is obvious that according to John 4:24 our internal worship must be given "in spirit," in our spirits, arising out of our inner hearts. It cannot be just from our mouths or hands, it must be "spiritual" and not "carnal" (Philippians 3:3). It must be the expression of all our "heart, soul, strength, and mind" (Luke 10:27). Worship cannot be simply by rote or given absentmindedly. Our internal worship must come from the undivided attention of our hearts.

Where does internal worship take us?

Even though the above may seem a strange question, true internal worship is supra-dimensional because when we worship God in our spirits, we are enabled by the Holy Spirit to enter into the dimension of heaven itself.

The Scriptures tell us that when we worship God we are translated to the throne of God and worship Him in the presence of all the angelic hosts and departed saints. Our worship blends into the worship going on in heaven. It is as if we had left the four dimensional world in which we live and have been translated to heaven itself.

Notice carefully *where* true worship takes place according to the following Scriptures:

Since then we have a great high priest who has passed through the heavens, Jesus the Son of God, let us hold fast our confession. For we do not have a high priest who cannot sympathize with our weaknesses, but one who has been tempted in all things as we are, yet without sin. Let us therefore draw near with confidence to the throne of grace, that we may receive mercy and may find grace to help in time of need *(Hebrews 4:14-16).*

Since therefore, brethren, we have confidence to enter the holy place by the blood of Jesus, by a new and living way which He inaugurated for us through the veil, that is, His flesh, and since we have a great priest over the house of God, let us draw near with a sincere heart in full assurance of faith, having our hearts sprinkled clean from an evil conscience and our bodies washed with pure water *(Hebrews 10:19-22).*

For you have not come to a mountain that may be touched and to a blazing fire, and to darkness and gloom and whirlwind, and to the blast of a trumpet and the sound of words which sound was such that those who heard begged that no further word should be spoken to them. For they could not bear the command, "If even a beast touches the mountain, it will be stoned." And so terrible was the sight that Moses said, "I am full of fear and trembling."

> But you have come to Mount Zion and to the city of the living God, the heavenly Jerusalem, and to myriads of angels, to the general assembly and church of the first-born who are enrolled in heaven, and to God, the Judge of all, and to the spirits of righteous men made perfect, and to Jesus, the mediator of a new covenant, and to the sprinkled blood, which speaks better than the blood of Abel *(Hebrews 12:18-24).*

In the above passages we are told that when we worship God we are brought into His presence in heaven and join the worship of all those in heaven. The illustration in Hebrews 12 is crucial to this concept of worship.

The belief that our worship is united to the worship going on in heaven explains why David could command the angelic hosts to join him in his worship of God.

> Bless the Lord, you His angels, mighty in strength, who perform His word, obeying the voice of His word! Bless the Lord, all you His hosts, you who serve Him, doing His will *(Psalm 103:20-21).*

> Praise the Lord! Praise the Lord from the heavens; praise Him in the heights! Praise Him, all His angels; praise Him all His hosts! *(Psalm 148:1-2).*

How often have the hosts of heaven joined us in our worship services? How often have we exhorted them to worship God with us? Perhaps the reason is that we do not have an awareness of the true "other worldly" character of worship. Worship is to be a "happening." It is a dynamic encounter between redeemed sinners and the Lord of the universe and all the hosts of heaven.

What is the foundation of internal worship? On what grounds or basis is our worship offered to God?

Internal worship is a spiritual privilege purchased for every believer by the precious blood of Christ. It is thus a birthright of every child of God. Its foundation is the atoning work of Christ.

> For through Him we both have our access in one Spirit to the Father *(Ephesians 2:18)*.

> Since therefore, brethren, we have confidence to enter the holy place by the blood of Jesus, by a new and living way which He inaugurated for us through the veil, that is His flesh, and since we have a great priest over the house of God, let us draw near with a sincere heart in full assurance of faith, having our hearts sprinkled clean from an evil conscience and our bodies washed with pure water *(Hebrews 10:19-22)*.

Our worship is acceptable to God only if it is offered through Christ and cleansed by Christ. His blood and heavenly intercession make our worship acceptable.

The Scriptures tell us quite bluntly that our worship is always tainted by our sin. Even though we are trying to worship God, our sins render our worship unacceptable. It is only through Christ's work that we can worship God acceptably.

In the Old Testament, Joshua the high priest needed cleansing before his worship was acceptable.

> Then he showed me Joshua the high priest standing before the angel of the Lord, and Satan standing at his right hand to accuse him and the Lord said to Satan, "The Lord rebuke you, Satan! Indeed, the Lord who has chosen Jerusalem rebuke you! Is this not a brand plucked from the fire?" Now Joshua was clothed with filthy garments and standing before the angel. And he spoke and said to those who were standing before him saying, "Remove the filthy garments from him." Again he said to him, "See, I have taken your iniquity away from you and will clothe you with festal robes." Then I said, "Let them put a clean turban on his head." So they put a clean turban on his head and clothed him with garments while the angel of the Lord was standing by *(Zechariah 3: 1-5).*

This is why the priests of Haggai's day needed to be reminded that their worship was defiled because they were sinners.

> On the twenty-fourth of the ninth month, in the second year of Darius, the word of the

Lord came to Haggai the prophet saying, "Thus says the Lord of hosts, 'Ask now the priests for a ruling: If a man carries holy meat in the fold of his garment, and touches bread with this fold, or cooked food, wine, oil, or any other food, will it become holy?' " And the priests answered and said, "no." Then Haggai said, "If one who is unclean from a corpse touches any of these, will the latter become unclean?" And the priests answered and said, "It will become unclean." Then Haggai answered and said, " 'So is this people. And so is this nation before Me,' declares the Lord, 'and so is every work of their hands; and what they offer there is unclean' " *(Haggai 2:10-14).*

In the New Testament, the apostle Peter clearly points out the necessity of Christ's atoning work to make our worship acceptable to God.

You, also, as living stones, are being built up as a spiritual house for a holy priesthood, to offer up spiritual sacrifices acceptable to God through Jesus Christ *(1 Peter 2:5).*

This truth should humble us. We cannot offer perfect and sinless worship to God until we die or Christ returns. We need to remind ourselves continually that we are utterly dependent upon Christ's blood and righteousness to make our worship acceptable.

Because of man's sinful nature, only the true believer can worship God acceptably (Romans 8:5-8; Proverbs 15:8). Since every believer is a priest of the Most High God, the true Christian can worship God acceptably (1 Peter 2:5; Hebrews 13:15).

There is a prescribed way to offer our worship. John 4:24 states that our worship must be "in truth" as well as "in spirit." This means that our internal worship is to be in conformity to Scripture for "Thy Word is truth" (John 17:17). We cannot simply make up our own worship any way we please. We must worship "in truth" because in every age God tells man how and in what way God is to be worshiped. He never leaves us to our own devices.

We need also to point out that our worship must be "by the Spirit" (Ephesians 2:18). The apostle Paul states,

> For we are the true circumcision, who worship in the Spirit of God and glory in Christ Jesus and put no confidence in the flesh *(Philippians 3:3)*.

Our worship is totally dependent upon the work of the Spirit as well as upon the atonement of Christ. Even prayer must be "in the Spirit" (Jude 20). The filling of the Holy Spirit is not a luxury for a few super-sanctified saints. It is not even a wild mystical extravagance. In Scripture, the filling of the Spirit is a practical induement with *power* in order to do the will of God. In Ephesians 5:18—6:9, the filling of the

Spirit is revealed as obedience in every area of life. It means power to worship (5:19-20); power to submit to each other (5:21); power to develop marriage harmony (5:22-23); power to raise children for Christ (6:1-4); power to have good employee-employer relationship (6:5-9).

The filling of the Spirit reveals itself in the life of a believer by practical everyday obedience to God's Word. We should never think that we are filled with the Spirit just because we have an emotional experience. Obedience and worship are the true signs of the Spirit-filled life.

How do we become Spirit-filled? Jesus told us how:

> If you then, being evil, know how to give good gifts to your children, how much more shall your heavenly Father give the Holy Spirit to those who ask Him? *(Luke 11:13).*

When we worship God in private, with our family or in church, we should begin simply by asking God to give us the filling of His Spirit to enable us to worship Him. Then we should take Him at His Word, and thank Him for filling us.

There is only One Being who is worthy of our worship. We are to worship the Triune God of Father, Son and Holy Spirit. This follows the trinitarian worship of the hosts of heaven (Isaiah 6:3; Revelation 4:8; 5:8-10, 12-14).

The Father desires to be worshiped (John 4:23-24). The Son is to be worshiped as well (John 5:23; 9:38; 1 Corinthians 1:2; Revelation 5:12-13).

The worship of the Holy Spirit can be established through 2 Corinthians 13:14 and Romans 15:30 where Paul refers to our love for and fellowship with the Holy Spirit.

In this light, we Christians must become very vocal against the idolatry which is being practiced today. The Hare Krishnas fall down and worship idols of stone and wood. The disciples of Transcendental Meditation worship their guru. The Satanists worship the devil. Some people worship statues of the saints or Mary. All these things are idolatrous and transgress the first and second commandments, which say:

> You shall have no other gods before Me. You shall not make for yourself an idol, or any likeness of what is in heaven above or on the earth beneath or in the water under the earth. You shall not worship them or serve them; for I, the Lord your God, am a jealous God, visiting the iniquity of the fathers on the children, on the third and the fourth generations of those who hate Me, but showing lovingkindness to thousands, to those who love Me and keep My commandments *(Exodus 20:3-6).*

Our answer to the modern idolators who are increasing in the land is found in the words of Jesus when Satan promised Him the kingdoms of the world if He would only fall down and worship him:

Then Jesus said to him, "Begone Satan! For it is written, 'You shall worship the Lord your God, and serve Him only' " *(Matthew 4:10)*.

The following diagram points out four things that happen in worship:

I. Certain things must be present in our hearts

Love
Joy
Adoration
Wonder
Awe
Reverence
Marvel
Admiration
Humility
Brokenness
Pride of God
Filial affection

II. We are saying or thinking certain things about God

We are praising, exalting, magnifying and lauding God for what He is in His being and for His mighty acts in creation, providence and redemption. We tell Him, we tell ourselves and we tell all creation that God is:
Good in His Being
Great in His power
Wonderful in His acts
Fearful in His judgment
Holy in His character
Loving in His mercies
Kind in His dealings
Glorious in all things

III. God's glory is being increased

While the intrinsic or essential glory of God is infinite and does not increase or decrease, God's acquired glory is increased by the free and true worship rendered to God by angelic beings and by redeemed humanity.

IV. God is responding

God gives grace, mercy and peace to enable us to live an obedient life. He blesses us as we bless Him.

Internal worship is the heart or soul of true worship. God will reject our external worship if it does not correspond to what is really in our hearts and minds. We must worship God in our heart by the Spirit according to the truth of Scripture through the work of Christ. Our worship is to be given to the Triune God—Father, Son and Holy Spirit—before whom and in whom we live and move and have our being. To Him be the glory forevermore. Amen.

Chapter Five
Public Worship: the Congregation

We now come in our study to the most controversial aspect of biblical worship. While few if any churches have experienced controversy due to differences over *internal* worship, many churches have experienced great controversy over differences as to how the worship service should be ordered and what should be and should not be allowed in the *external* worship of God. Since we are dealing with such a sensitive issue, we must closely follow the Word of God and let it judge our ideas of what is right and wrong in the public worship of God.

In chapter 4, external or public worship was defined as "the outward visible or audible acts of worship which are done in public worship. It is composed of the forms, ceremonies, liturgies, orders of service and various ingredients in the meeting which make up congregational worship."

Having examined in previous chapters what the heart and mind do in worship, we will examine what the body does in worship. How should we visibly and publicly worship God in the assembly of the saints?

There are two basic and foundational principles of external worship. First, we must prepare our hearts for public worship. If we do not prepare our hearts for worship, we will not be able to participate in true worship. This will result in the absence of God's presence, and there will be no realization of joy in worship. In place of joy, we will experience boredom, dullness, passivity, daydreaming and, perhaps, even sleepiness. But God has revealed in His Word that public worship should be a rewarding experience. Did not David declare that "in Thy presence is fulness of joy; in Thy right hand hand there are pleasures forever"? (Psalm 16:11). For this reason the psalmist said, "My heart is steadfast, O God; I will sing, I will sing praises, even with my soul" (Psalm 108:1). David was determined to worship and nothing would be allowed to hinder him. He had prepared his heart for worship.

Second, public worship is to be ordered by what has been historically called "the regulative principle of worship."

Three conflicting approaches to worship have developed. The first position sets forth the concept that whatever is not forbidden in Scripture is allowed. Thus total freedom in public worship is established by simply placing the burden of proof on anyone who objects to something being done. This approach was the basis for justifying such things as the mass, prayers to Mary and the saints, the rosary, incense, candles, etc.

This first approach is clearly unbiblical for both the Old and New Testaments state that God is to be worshiped according to His directions. We do not have the freedom to do as we please in worship. Indeed, the Bible would have to be a thousand volumes if God had to forbid everything the mind of man could invent. Instead, God has explicitly stated in Scripture by way of precept, command and example that whatever is not commanded is forbidden.

God has repeatedly told His people that they were forbidden to add to or subtract from the worship which He had revealed (Deuteronomy 4:1-2; 12:29-32; Isaiah 8:20; Revelation 22:18-19).

When Nadab and Abihu "offered strange fire before the Lord, which He had not commanded them, fire came out from the presence of the Lord and consumed them" (Leviticus 10:1-2).

Even though God had not forbidden the kind of fire they wanted to offer, it was rejected because it was not the kind of fire directly commanded by God.

Korah, Dathan and Abiram all tried to institute things which were neither commanded nor forbidden by God (Numbers 16:1-40). When they attempted unauthorized worship, the ground opened up and swallowed them, and fire went forth and devoured their followers.

When King Uzziah went into the temple and offered incense to God, even though he may have felt that God did not directly forbid kings from doing so, he was struck with leprosy for violating what was revealed (2 Chronicles 26: 16-21).

With such Old Testament examples, it is no wonder when we come to the New Testament, we find Jesus commanding that worship must be "in truth" and teaching that "God's word is truth" (John 4:24; cf. John 17:17). According to Christ, worship must be structured by God's Word.

In John 4, Christ did not approve of the Samaritan innovations in worship but gave validity only to the revealed worship of Israel (John 4:19-24). He clearly commissioned His disciples to teach "whatever I have commanded you," not "whatever I have not forbidden" (Matthew 28:20). Christ's commission clearly limits the essentials of worship to what He commanded.

Because of the plain teaching of Scripture, the Reformers such as Calvin developed what we now call "the regulative principle of worship." This principle states: For the essentials of worship, only what God has commanded in Scripture is to be allowed. Nothing is to be viewed as essential to divine worship if it is not commanded in Scripture. The non-essential aspects of worship are left up to the freedom of the conscience, and the edification of the church.

Calvin and some of the other Reformers sought to develop a balance between form and freedom in worship. The following chart shows the balance they set forth.

FORM	The essentials of worship must be clearly commanded in Scripture. All else is forbidden.
FREEDOM	The non-essentials of worship must conform to the general principles of the freedom of the conscience and the edification of the church.

Calvin further expounded:

> I approve only those human constitutions which are founded upon God's authority, drawn from Scripture, and, therefore, wholly divine. . . .

> I mean that the Lord has in His sacred oracles faithfully embraced and clearly expressed both the whole sum of true righteousness, and all aspects of the worship of His majesty, and whatever was necessary to salvation; therefore, in these the Master alone is to be heard. But because He did not will in outward discipline and ceremonies to prescribe in detail what we ought to do (because He foresaw that this depended upon the state of the times, and He did not deem one form suitable for all ages), here we must take refuge in those general rules which He has given, that whatever the necessity of the church will require for order and decorum should be tested against these. Lastly, because He has taught nothing specifically, and because these

things are not necessary to salvation, and for the upbuilding of the church ought to be variously accommodated to the customs of each nation and age, it will be fitting (as the advantage of the church will require) to change and abrogate traditional practices and to establish new ones. Indeed, I admit that we ought not to charge into innovation rashly, suddenly, for insufficient cause. But love will best judge what may hurt or edify; and if we let love be our guide, all will be safe. (John Calvin, *Institutes of Christian Religion,* Vol. II, pp. 30-32.)

According to the Reformers, the essential aspects of worship must come only from the Scriptures. Neither the state nor the church can designate something as essential to worship if it is not commanded in the Scriptures.

What are the essentials of worship? The Scriptures require that singing, praying, preaching, giving, testifying and edification should comprise worship. We should also observe the two gospel ordinances of baptism and the Lord's Supper (Matthew 28:19-20; Acts 2:41-42, 46-47; 20:7; 1 Corinthians 11:20-33; 14:20-33; 16:2).

What are the non-essentials of worship? A non-essential element is something or some act whose presence or absence does not validate or invalidate worship. It is a matter of convenience, circumstance, culture and aesthetic taste. They refer to where, when and how we worship. Whether you worship in a barn or a cathedral is unimportant. A choir, special music, pews, a church bell or special clothing are non-essentials.

The Reformation position is reaffirmed through Paul's dealings with a church which was confused on how to order the non-essential aspects of worship. He pointed them to the general principles which guide Christian freedom and the edification of the church. He asked the Corinthians to judge the non-essential aspects of worship by answering the following questions:

- Does this action promote order or confusion? *(1 Corinthians 14:33, 40)*
- Is it decent and proper? *(14:40)*
- Does it edify the Body? *(14:5, 12, 26)*
- Is it what love wants? *(14:1)*
- Does it glorify God? *(10:31)*
- Does it contradict Scripture? *(4:6)*

Paul does not refer the Corinthians to a prescribed order of service revealed from God. He points them instead to a mature and responsible exercise of their priestly freedom in the non-essential aspects of worship.

While the first position taught total freedom, and the second position sought to develop a balance between form and freedom, a third position arose in 17th-century England.

Some of the Puritans, in fighting the superstitions and idolatry of their age, went to the extreme of reducing the worship of God to the absolute minimum of what was commanded by Scripture. Their fear of the abuse of freedom in worship led them to embrace only the form of the essentials. They reduced the worship of God to the bare bones of a long sermon and a few hymns.

Dr. J.I. Packer points out the extremes of this third position in the following statement:

> German, Swiss and English Reformers held common basic principles about worship. They agreed that Christian worship must express man's reception of, and response to, evangelical truth, and they were substantially in agreement as to what that truth was. They agreed in analyzing worship as an exercise of mind and heart in praise, thanksgiving, prayer, confession of sin, trust in God's promises, and the hearing of God's Word, read and preached. They were in agreement also as to the nature and number of the gospel sacraments, and their place in the church's worship. They took the same view of the office of the Christian minister in leading the worship of the congregation. They agreed also that each church, or federation of churches ("every particular or national church," as Article XXXIV puts it) is responsible for settling the details of its own worship in accordance with the apostolic principle that all must be done "unto edifying" *(1 Corinthians 14:26)*, and that as a means to that end everything must be done "decently and in order" *(14:40)*. Finally, they were all agreed that

each church has liberty (the presupposition of its responsibility) to arrange its worship in the best way adapted to edify its own worshipers, in the light of their state, background and needs; so that they all took it for granted that the worship of varied churches in varying pastoral situations would vary in detail. The only real differences regarding worship between any of the first generation of Reformers were differences of personal judgment as to what would edify and what would not—differences of the kind reflected in Calvin's judgment that the second Edwardian Prayer Book of 1552 contained *multas tolerabiles ineptias* ("many bearable pieces of foolishness"), or in the troubles at Frankfurt in 1554, when the "Coxian" group of exiles adhered to the 1552 Prayer Book as being sufficiently sound and edifying, while the "Knoxians" felt obliged to abandon it in favor of an alternative order drawn up on the Geneva pattern.

The idea that direct biblical warrant, in the form of precept or precedent, is required to sanction every item included in the public worship of God was in fact a Puritan innovation, which crystallized out in the course of the prolonged debates that followed the Elizabethan settlement. It is an idea distinct from the principle that tainted ceremonies, which hide the truth from worshipers and buttress superstitious error, should be dropped, as both dishonoring God and impeding edification. On this latter principle all the English Reformers were agreed from the start, as the 1549 Prayer Book, Preface "Of Ceremonies" shows. . . . But this new principle went further, declaring that no justification of non-biblical rites and ceremonies in worship as convenient means to biblically prescribed ends could in the nature of the case be valid (in other words, that the line taken in the Preface "Of Ceremonies" was wrong); all ceremonies must have direct biblical warrant, or they were impious intrusions. The same principle was applied to church government. The attempt to put the Puritan ideal of church life and worship on to this footing led to some curiosities of argument, such as the "proof" that two services a Sunday were obligatory, from Numbers 28:4-9, which prescribes two burnt offerings each Sabbath; or the "proof" that catechizing was a duty, from "hold fast the form of sound words" *(2 Timothy 1:13)*; or the "proof" of the necessity of the controversial "prophesyings" (area preaching meetings, at which several ministers spoke successively on the same passage of Scripture), from 1 Corinthians 14:31 ("ye may all prophesy one by one, that all may learn and all may be comforted"). Much of this can be cogently defended, in terms of the principle that all things must be done unto edifying, but it is hard to regard these biblical arguments as anything like conclusive.

It should also be noticed that when the Puritans singled out some of the *ineptiae* of the Prayer Book as intolerable; when they challenged the principle that each church has liberty to ordain non-biblical ceremonies in worship where these seem conducive to edification and reverence; when they repudiated all set prayers; when they rejected kneeling in public worship, the Christian year, weekly Communion, and the practice of confirmation; they were not in fact reverting to Calvin, but departing from him, though, as Horton Davies says (*The Worship of the English Puritans,* p. 48), it is doubtful whether they realized this. (J.I. Packer, "The Puritan Approach to Worship," *Diversity in Unity,* Papers read at the Puritan and Reformed Studies Conference, Dec. 1963, pp. 4-5).

This third position is further refuted by the following observations:

If everything in the worship service must have a Scripture text, why doesn't the New Testament give us a set order of service? Where are the regulations and rules? It is only obvious that in the New Testament such non-essentials are left up to Christian liberty and the edification of the church.

This position is retrogressive in seeking to

arrange Christian worship according to Old Testament Law.

During the age of the Old Testament, the people of God were viewed as "children" and were under bondage to the "beggarly elements" of the Law (Galatians 3:23; 4:1-5). But during the New Testament age, we are no longer viewed as such. Instead, we are viewed as full sons and daughters who are to exercise our freedom in a responsible way (Galatians 3:23-25; 4:4-7; 5:1, 13; 2 Corinthians 3:6, 17).

It is impossible consistently to carry out this position. It ultimately leads to legalism, absurdity and dead orthodoxy.

To those who tell us today that we cannot have a choir or special music because we do not have a verse in the New Testament where such things are commanded we must ask, "Where is there a verse for the pews you sit on? Where is the New Testament passage for having a hymnal? Where is the text for an organ or piano?"

What we need above all things in the public worship of God is a balance between form and freedom.

The three conflicting positions on external or public worship can now be summarized in the following chart:

Focus	TOTAL FREEDOM	FORM AND FREEDOM	TOTAL FORM
Result	Idolatry, license, superstition	A balance in worship	Legalism, bondage, dead orthodoxy
Basis	Whatever is not forbidden is allowed.	For essentials look to biblical form; for non-essentials seek the edification of the church.	Everything in worship must have a Scripture verse to validate it.

Chapter Six

Public Worship: New Testament Precedents

Having reviewed the basic principles of biblical worship, we will now examine the characteristics or attributes of New Testament worship. We will answer the questions, "What should a New Testament worship service look like? What should apply today?"

The 10 points throughout this chapter are to be viewed as general guidelines and not as an order of service. How these 10 points will manifest themselves in any given congregation depends on the culture and circumstances of that church. But they are a guide to judge how close a church has come to full biblical worship.

1. Biblical worship is congregational

Too often it is assumed that worship is a spectator sport. The congregation sits passively and watches the professionals "up front" worship God. The choir sings, the pastor prays and preaches and the congregation sings a few hymns, but for the most part, the congregation is passive. Is this biblical?

In the Old Testament age, worship actively involved the congregation. Dr. R. Girdlestone, in his famous *Synonyms of the Old Testament,* comments:

> Turning to the more directly religious usage of the word *shachah,* it may be observed that the worship of God was to be carried out by the people themselves, and was not done for them by the priest (p. 216).

Throughout the Old Testament, the people were involved in the following:

- Standing and praising God with shouts, prayers, exaltations, etc. *(Nehemiah 9:5; Ezra 3:11-13; Psalm 5:11; 32:11; 35:27; 47:1; 132:9, 16; Zephaniah 3:14; 2 Samuel 6:15; Zechariah 4:7)*
- Singing praise to God *(Psalm 9:11; 21:13; 30:4; 33:1-2; 47:6-7; 68:4)*
- Playing musical instruments during praise *(Psalm 150; 2 Samuel 6:5; 1 Chronicles 13:8; 2 Chronicles 20:26-28)*
- Sharing testimonies *(Psalm 22:22, 25; 35:18; 40:9-10)*
- Fasting *(Nehemiah 9:1; Ezra 8:23)*
- Lifting hands in worship *(Nehemiah 8:6; Psalm 28:2; 63:4; 134:2; 141:2; Lamentations 3:40-41)*
- Clapping *(Psalm 47:1)*
- Dancing *(Psalm 150:4)*
- Giving tithes and offerings *(Malachi 3: 8-10)*

- Reading responsively *(Psalm 136)*
- Offering special sacrifices *(Leviticus 1-5)*
- Shouting Amen *(Nehemiah 5:13; 8:5; Deuteronomy 25:15-26; 1 Chronicles 16:36)*
- Listening to Scripture read, taught and preached *(Nehemiah 8:1-8; Ecclesiastes 12: 9-11)*

Worship, to the Old Testament saints, was not a dreary passive experience. It was a dynamic encounter with the living God. It was congregational in its very essence.

Worship in the New Testament church was just as congregational as in the Old Testament because it grew out of the worship of the synagogue.

Ralph P. Martin points out in *Worship in the Early Church* that the worship of the synagogue was congregational in format. The people took an active part in praise, prayer and preaching. It was not a passive, spectator experience. This also explains how Jesus could read and expound Isaiah 61:1 in Nazareth and how Paul could preach in the synagogues (Luke 4:16-21; Acts 17: 1-3).

It is no wonder then that the worship services described in the New Testament were decidedly congregational. *The International Standard Bible Encyclopedia* supports this in the following comment:

> First Corinthians gives rather full data for the worship in this free and enthusiastic

church. It appears that there were two meetings, a public and a private. The public worship was open, informal and missionary as well as edificatory. The unconverted, inquirers and others, were expected to be present, and were frequently converted in the meeting *(1 Corinthians 14:24)*. It resembled much more closely an evangelical "prayer and conference meeting" of today than our own formal church services.

Any . . . member was free to take part as the Spirit might prompt, especially in the line of his particular "spiritual gift" from God, although one individual might have several, as Paul himself. Largely developed on synagogue lines, but with a freedom and spirit the latter must have greatly lacked, it was composed of: (1) Prayer by several, each followed by the congregational Amen. (2) Praise consisting of hymns composed by one or another of the brethren, or coming down from the earlier days of Christian, perhaps Jewish, history, like the Benedictus, the Magnificat, the Nunc dimittis.

Portions of these newer hymns seem to be imbedded here and there in the New Testament, as in Revelation 11:17; 15:3; also "He who was revealed in the flesh, was vindicated in the spirit, beheld by angels, proclaimed among the nations, believed on in the world, taken up in glory" *(1 Timothy 3:16)*. Praise also might take the form of individual testimony, not in metrical form

(1 Corinthians 14:16). (3) Reading of the Scripture must have followed, according to the synagogue model. Paul presupposes an acquaintance with the Old Testament Scriptures and the facts of Jesus' life, death, resurrection. Instructions to read certain epistles in the churches indicate the same. (4) Instruction, as in 1 Corinthians 2:7; 6:5, was teaching for edification. (These passages, however, may not have this specific reference.) (5) Prophesying when men, moved by the Holy Spirit, gave utterance to His message. At Corinth these crowded on one another, so that Paul had to command them to speak one at a time. (6) Following this, as some believe, came the "speaking with tongues," perhaps fervent and spontaneous prayers "so rugged and disjointed that the audience for the most part could not understand" until someone interpreted. The speaking with tongues, however, comprised praise as well as prayer *(1 Corinthians 14:16),* and the whole subject is enshrouded in mystery. (7) The meeting closed with the benediction and with the "kiss of peace."

The private service may have followed the other, but seems move likely to have been in the evening, the other in the morning. The disciples met in one place and ate together a meal of their own providing, the agape, or love feast, symbolizing their union and fellowship, preceded or followed by prayers and perhaps interspersed by hymns. Then followed the Lord's Supper itself, according to the directions of the apostle *(1 Corinthians 11:23-28)*. (Vol. V., p. 3112).

While there are elements of the above article which can be debated, no New Testament scholar denies the congregational worship of the early church.

Since the worship of the early church grew out of the temple and the synagogue, many Hebraic forms of worship were carried over into Christian worship: praising God with shouts, singing praise to God, sharing testimonies, fasting, lifting hands in worship, giving offerings, shouting Amen and listening to Scripture taught, read and preached.

The early church dropped the offering of temple sacrifices because Christ had fulfilled their typological meaning (Hebrews 10:18). They also abandoned the Sabbath, circumcision and all the other ceremonial laws (Colossians 2:16-17; Galatians 3:23-29; 4:1-7; 5:1-6; Philippians 3:2-3).

No direct mention in the New Testament is made of musical instruments or of the clapping of hands, but musical instruments were used in the temple and synagogues where the early church first met. Calvin and some other commentators also see the use of musical instruments in the root meaning of the word "psalm" in Colossians 3:16. The same holds true for the clapping of hands in worship. Since these were ways in which the disciples had worshiped God all their lives, we must begin with the assumption that unless Christ or the apostles explicitly forbade them, such things would continue in practice. Today the burden of proof falls upon those who forbid the people of God from clapping their hands or playing musical instruments in the worship service.

The early church added some distinctly Christian elements to worship: observing baptism and the Lord's Supper (Acts 2:4, 42; 20:7), worshiping on Sunday and worshiping not only to glorify God but also to edify the church (1 Corinthians 14:19-31; Acts 15:32; 21:4; Romans 12:13; James 5:16; Hebrews 10:24-25; Galatians 6:2).

The early church discovered that it could not fulfill all its New Covenant responsibilities in one service. So it held two meetings. The morning meeting centered on the teaching of the eldership and resulted in vital learning experiences. The evening meeting centered in mutual edification. It resulted in dynamic relational experiences when the members of the Body ministered to each other. Some commentators feel that First Corinthians is discussing these house-church meetings which centered in mutual and open worship. It is impossible to do everything in one service which the New Testament points out as being "Body Life." Therefore, two services are needed.

We need to recapture the dynamic of scriptural congregational worship in order to experience the blessing of God upon our churches. It is interesting to note that historically whenever true revival came upon churches, the degree of congregational involvement in worship increased tremendously. It is a sign of God's blessing.

2. Biblical worship is charismatic

The word "charismatic" is a good biblical word. It comes from the Greek word for "gift." In this sense all Christians are "charismatic," because they have received the "charisma" of God which is eternal life in Christ Jesus our Lord (Romans 6:23).

While charisma refers in its first sense to the gift of eternal life, it also refers to the gifts of the Holy Spirit which He has distributed in the church in order that all may minister as the priests of God.

Just as there are no "spiritless" Christians, there are no "giftless" Christians. This is why the apostle Paul and the apostle Peter both assumed if someone was a Christian, he or she had a part in the mutual ministry of edification in the Body because God had given him or her at least one gift (Romans 12:3-8; 1 Peter 4:8-11).

We must hasten to add that even though a person received a basic gift at the new birth, he or she must not be content with this one gift but go on to seek other ministry and manifestation gifts as well (1 Corinthians 13:31; 14:1).

How are the spiritual gifts to be used? The

primary focus is always the edification of the church. Paul wrote:

> Now there are varieties of gifts, but the same Spirit. And there are varieties of ministries, and the same Lord. And there are varieties of effects, but the same God who works all things in all persons. But to each one is given the manifestation of the Spirit for the common good. For to one is given the word of wisdom through the Spirit, and to another the word of knowledge according to the same Spirit; to another faith by the same Spirit, and to another gifts of healing by the one Spirit, and to another the effecting of miracles, and to another prophecy, and to another the distinguishing of spirits, to another various kinds of tongues, and to another the interpretation of tongues. But one and the same Spirit works all these things, distributing to each one individually just as He wills *(1 Corinthians 12:4-11).*

> Pursue love, yet desire earnestly spiritual gifts, but especially that you may prophesy. For one who speaks in a tongue does not speak to men, but to God; for no one understands, but in his Spirit he speaks mysteries. But one who prophesies speaks to men for edification and exhortation and consolation. One who speaks in a tongue edifies himself; but one who prophesies edifies the church *(1 Corinthians 14:1-4).*

In the light of these and other passages, there should be opportunity in the life of every local church for the members to exercise their gifts. Presently, only the pastor exercises his gift. One man and his one or more gifts carries the whole service. This is unscriptural.

Instead of seeking leaders with natural talents (i.e. abilities which they received through heredity), why not seek leaders who can minister to the Body through spiritual gifts (i.e. abilities which they received from the Holy Spirit)?

It is to be feared that our past emphasis on "talent" revealed our ignorance and fear of spiritual gifts. It is also obvious that we are in a deplorable state today because our leadership has been traditionally selected on the basis of "talent" instead of spiritual might and spiritual gifts. Therefore, we must start emphasizing the importance of the Holy Spirit's equipping all the people of God with His gifts in order for mutual edification to take place. The leaders and the congregation have been equipped by God to minister. Let us use the gifts which God has given to the Body of Christ.

3. Biblical worship is kerygmatic

By kerygmatic we mean that worship is always structured by and responsive to the proclamation of Scripture. The teaching, reading, preaching and discussion of the Word of God should play a vital role in public worship.

Now, on the basis of what has already been said about preaching sometimes supplanting mutual edification and open worship, we must emphasize that the proclamation of the Word is vital and essential for worship.

There are two extremes concerning the place of preaching which must be avoided at all costs.

In one extreme, preaching is exalted to be the whole purpose of meeting together. The pastor preaches a long sermon and the people of God are conditioned to think that their primary religious obligation to God and their neighbor has been fulfilled if they sit quietly during the sermon. Such things as the singing of hymns and the collection of money are viewed as necessary evils best rushed through as quickly as possible in order to get to the real reason for assembling—the sermon.

Many well-meaning pastors are often unconsciously drawn to this kind of position. They will not allow anyone else to participate in the service. They often look with horror at the teaching of "Body life" and preach against it with vigor because in their mind it threatens the "centrality of preaching." Their people know little of congregational worship. They are afraid that things might get out of control if the people were allowed open worship or testimony times. Everything is run like a well-oiled machine. The church is absolutely safe from any revivals or charismatic intrusions. It sleeps secure in its dogmatic slumber.

At the other extreme are those who exalt mutual edification and open worship to the exclusion of preaching. They feel that they only need sharing and fellowship. They believe that anyone in the Body can teach, prophesy and edify so why have a pastor preach the Word? Why have a sermon? They fail to grasp the absolute necessity and centrality of the authoritative proclamation of the Word of God.

Some of these groups only emphasize open worship and the mutual exercise of spiritual gifts. Some have gone into drama and dance as substitutions for the proclamation of the Word of God.

As with the first extreme, while some of the things being done are biblically proper, it is what has been left out that is wrong. We should not exclude "Body life," or preaching. Both have their time and place in the life of the church. These extremes are manifestations of the pendulum propensity of the depravity of the human heart. May God grant that we will develop a biblical approach to the place of preaching.

4. Biblical worship is open to the Holy Spirit

The great Baptist preacher, Charles Spurgeon, felt so strongly about being open to the Holy Spirit's changing his message or interrupting the service that he decided not to preach any series of expository sermons through a given book in the Bible lest he preach a sermon simply because it was next in line in a series of messages instead of receiving a fresh word from God. While he may have gone to extremes in his feelings against expository preaching, he nevertheless saw the importance of being open to the Holy Spirit's leading.

The early church was open to the Spirit's leading as an essential part of public worship, and this must not be viewed as a temporary response to the presence of an uncompleted canon. Perhaps an examination of the elements of New Testament worship will help us to see how important it is to remain open to the Holy Spirit.

We too often assume that God will only speak through the pastor. We cannot assume that God gives only the pastor the Word of the Lord every Sunday out of the year. Indeed, we have all heard sermons which we felt did not come from God. It is obvious that there will be times when God wants someone else to preach. The real problem is that the pastor, due to insecurity, is not willing to give up his pulpit. And the people have been trained not to think of themselves as being worthy to proclaim God's Word.

How different was the early church! The classic passages such as Acts 8:4 and 1 Corinthians 14:23-33 have withstood all attempts to restrict preaching to the ordained clergy. Hebrews 5:12 and Colossians 3:16 are still in the Bible. The Lord wants to speak through *all* His people, not just the pastor.

On different occasions I as a pastor have told my congregation, "God did not give me the Word of the Lord for you today. I have sought the Lord earnestly and He has not given me a message. This means that He has given one or more of you the message for today. If God has laid a burden upon your heart with a teaching or an exhortation, please speak up." On every occasion one or more of the people of God stood and proclaimed the Word of the Lord with vigor and unction from on High.

When should the sermon be given? Sometimes the sermon should be at the beginning or in the middle instead of always at the end. The Holy Spirit should have the freedom to place the proclamation of the Word at the most edifying point of the service.

The key issue is whether we are really open to the Spirit's changing the order or the elements of the worship service. We must not be fossilized into a set order of service. God's frozen people need to become His chosen people who will allow Him to intervene in the worship service.

5. Biblical worship is edifying to all by all

The unique contribution of New Covenant worship to the worship of the Old Testament is that there must be an emphasis on doing those things in the worship service which *edify* the people of God (1 Corinthians 14:26; Ephesians 4:10-16).

We must never view public worship as a time for private exercises of devotion. It is not a selfish time where we are to exercise our gifts only for the benefit of our souls. Instead, we should seek the Lord as to how we can minister to and edify the people of God.

This biblical rule of edification should be used to judge all the programs in a church. Regardless of how time-honored or tradition-encrusted an activity or program may be, if it is not unto edification it should be discarded and something better put in its place. In order to search out the level of edification in your church, compare your church programs to the words of the apostle Paul:

Therefore it says, "When He ascended on high, He led captive a host of captives, and He gave gifts to men."

And He gave some as apostles, and some as prophets, and some as evangelists, and some as pastors and teachers, for the equipping of the saints for the work of service, to the building up of the body of Christ; until we all attain to the unity of the faith, and of the knowledge of the Son of God, to a mature man, to the measure of the stature which belongs to the fulness of Christ. As a result, we are no longer to be children, tossed here and there by waves, and carried about by every wind of doctrine, by the trickery of men, by craftiness in deceitful scheming; but speaking the truth in love, we are to grow up in all aspects unto Him, who is the head, even Christ, from whom the whole body, being fitted and held together by that which every joint supplies, according to the proper working of each individual part, causes the growth of the body for the building up of itself in love *(Ephesians 4:8, 11-16).*

6. *Biblical worship is dynamic and enthusiastic*

The worship services of the early church were not marked with the dullness, deadness and formality which characterizes many churches today. There was a dynamic quality in their worship which resulted in conversions, healed relationships and changed lives.

The people were enthusiastic because they were actively involved in the service. The service was open to the Spirit's leading and to the exercise of the gifts of the Spirit. There was expectation and excitement due to the necessity of looking to God for the success of the meeting. They were not content to go through rote forms and rituals in a passive, unthinking manner.

The benefits of joyous worship are many. One benefit is that this kind of worship will captivate the youth of a church. They will not be bored when God is worshiped with honest zeal and enthusiasm. Zeal and enthusiasm are always contagious and young people are quick to participate if they sense that what is going on is exciting.

7. *Biblical worship is God-centered*

Instead of going to church merely to hear a sermon or to exercise our spiritual gifts, we should recognize that true worship is "ministering to the Lord" (Acts 13:2).

The Old Testament word *a'bad* means "to wait on" or "to minister to," as a slave does his master. It was used as a word for worship because we are to serve the Lord or minister to Him.

This means that worship must be God-centered. To be God-centered, we must strive not to be self-conscious or people-conscious but God-conscious. We must strive to increase God's acquired glory.

The New Testament writers used the word *latreuo,* which is the Greek parallel to *a'bad,* in order to emphasize that true worship is ministering to the Lord. It is "our reasonable service of worship" (Romans 12:1-2).

The best way to teach people how to minister to the Lord is to have a time in the worship service where they can concentrate on Him and exalt Him as God. This necessitates open worship.

In traditional church services, things are arranged in such a way that someone is always talking, praying or singing up front, and no time is left for the people to offer pure spontaneous worship to God. This must be corrected if the people of God are to minister to the Lord.

8. Biblical worship is a balance between form and freedom

There are certain things which are not optional in worship. We cannot dispense with preaching, praying, singing or mutual edification. The essentials of worship constitute the immutable form and core of true worship.

Yet, we have freedom in the non-essentials of

worship. If some want to have special music, God bless them. If some do not, God bless them, too!

When we turn an essential element into a non-essential or a non-essential into an essential we create an imbalance. Some forms of imbalance may work against true worship.

9. Biblical worship is physical as well as intellectual

If we had lived in Corinth in the first century, we would have noticed a significant difference between the worship in the Greek temples and the worship in the Jewish synagogues and Christian churches.

The Greeks deified the mind because it was related to the world of ideas. The body was evil because it was related to matter. The Greeks would come into their temples to listen in silence to the oracle or the priest speak. The emphasis was on silence and contemplation.

This was in contrast to the Jews and Christians who made noise when they worshiped. Since the body was not viewed as evil by the Scriptures, it was used in worship.

In the Old Testament, the word *shachah* meant to fall down prostrate. To the Hebrew mind the position of the body was an indication of the attitude of the heart. So they physically bowed down in worship (2 Chronicles 29:29; Nehemiah 8:6), lifted their hands to God (Psalm 63:1-5), clapped their hands (Psalm 47:1) and everyone prayed and praised at the same time

(2 Chronicles 29:28; Nehemiah 8:6; 9:1-5).

To the New Testament writers, the body as well as the mind was to be used in worship. They used the word *proskuneo* which means to fall down prostrate. It is the parallel to *shachah*. They physically bowed down to worship Jesus (Matthew 28:9; John 9:38). They also lifted their hands to God (1 Timothy 2:8).

We hasten to add that the apostolic practice of using the body in worship should not be dismissed as a meaningless cultural activity. For example, the lifting up of the hands to God is a means of true worship. That the Jews and Christians worshiped and prayed with palms held up and open to God is clear in the Scriptures. All early Christian art pictured Christ and His followers as praying or worshiping God with hands lifted up. Does this gesture have a meaning? Or, is it merely a cultural gesture?

The lifting up of the hands to God with palms held up and open has great significance:

First, it means that we are lifting up our hearts to God for grace and mercy (Lamentations 3:4).

Second, it means that we recognize the Lordship of God over all of our lives and respond to Him in humility (Psalm 63:4; Nehemiah 8:6).

Third, it is an act of worship in itself (Nehemiah 8:6; Psalm 134:2).

Fourth, it symbolizes our reaching out to God in prayer or supplication (1 Timothy 2:8; Psalm 28:2).

There are other reasons as well. It is obvious

that praying with hands lifted up to God has just as much significance today as in the Old Testament or New Testament. Today, there are many Christians who are worshiping God with hands uplifted. May more of God's people try this and other ancient forms of worship.

10. Biblical worship is Christ-glorifying

Authentic New Testament worship will involve the worship of Christ for He is God of very God as well as man of very man. It was the worship of Christ as God that separated the early Christians from the Jewish synagogue (1 Corinthians 1:2). And it is this same worship that separates the true Christians today from the forces of liberalism, the cults and the occult. Any worship that does not acknowledge the absolute deity of Christ is not Christian worship.

Christ is to receive equal honor with the Father, according to the apostle John.

> In order that all may honor the Son, even as they honor the Father *(John 5:23)*.

If Christ is not honored in worship, the Father will not receive worship.

> Whoever denies the Son does not have the Father; the one who confesses the Son has the Father also *(1 John 2:23)*.

The early historical records of Christian worship point out the worship of Christ as God. The Lord's Supper was misunderstood by pagan leaders as the "eating and drinking" of God. The early church focused its worship on the risen Lord because the glory of His person and the dignity of His work formed the very foundation of the church. Christ is to be at the center of all worship.

The following diagram illustrates the 10 attributes or earmarks of New Testament worship.

We should strive toward these goals in order to structure our worship according to the Scriptures. There is a growing movement among the people of God today to return to their biblical roots. May God use this study of worship to encourage His people to strive for the beauty of full New Testament worship.

Conclusion

As children of God we have a wonderful privilege and an awesome task set before us when we consider God's call to worship Him. We were created with the need and the ability to bow before our Creator and to give God the glory due Him. It is only as we do this that we can be fulfilled in our humanity. The health of our relationship with God will affect our relationship to everything else.

Our self-image requires the presence of God in our lives if we want to view ourself as God does.

Our relationship to our family depends upon our relationship to God. We cannot function as husbands, wives and children as God intended if we do not bow before the Lord of the universe.

Our relationship to society will be affected by our relationship to God. Our unique place as humans in the world cannot be understood except in terms of our relationship to the God who made us.

It is the vision of all of life as worship that gives beauty and significance to even the little things in life. When we are "holistic" Christians who view all of life as sacred, then and only then will a theistic world and life view be possible. We must learn that we "live and move and have our being in God" (Acts 17:28).

It is only as we Christians take hold of holistic

worship that the world will sit up and take notice. The sweet fragrance of worship should be everywhere. It should permeate all of society and culture.

This holistic vision begins with a personal encounter with the Lord Jesus Christ and issues in an entire life of worship. Let God's acquired glory be forever increased by the free worship of heaven and earth. Let the whole earth be filled with His Glory!

Suggested Reading

Martin, Ralph P. *Worship in the Early Church.* Grand Rapids: Eerdmans, 1975.

Ortland, Ann. *Up with Worship.* Glendale, Calif.: Regal Books, 1982.

Stedman, Ray. *Body Life.* Glendale, Calif.: Regal Books, 1972.

Snyder, Howard A. *The Problem of Wine Skins.* Downers Grove, Ill.: InterVarsity Press, 1979.